Praise for Brin

"With so many business
a sprinkle of something c.
this book has it. This is the first time ı ɪ ᴜ . ᴸ
that focuses on communication, values and being true
to yourself. The book reaffirms a lot of what I already
know but is a valuable reminder to me of what I have
learnt, particularly at times when I need support. I will
regularly refer to the checklists SJ has created because
in times of stress, we need sound, rational advice when
we are not thinking that way. I love the honesty in the
style of writing, and its simplicity. This stuff doesn't need
to be complicated, we just need to hear it from someone
in a way that works for us. And I shall no longer worry
about dropping one of my many balls, but simply and
calmly decide to put a few of them down and refocus."
K Huggins, Huggins Law

"Within a month of reading Bringing Human Back and
following the detailed exercises contained within it, I had
interviewed for and secured my dream job. Focussing
on the 'clarity' and 'control' that Bringing Human Back
hammers home enabled me to efficiently pin-point my
strengths and the client solutions I can offer, making
me much more confident in the product I can sell - me!"
N Knight-Wickens, Spencer West

"There are some great gems in there that make you go
"kerching"!" *S Ambasna, Nourish Food For Life*

"It's not just for those just setting up business, but as someone who has been in business for some time, it's something to return to time and time again." *J Knopf, Gander Media*

"It was a motivating and uplifting read encouraging people not to take any crap from the start of and then throughout their business journey." *H Cox, Helen Cox Marketing*

"If, like me, you're sick of the load of waffle you tend to come across in business books before seeing any valuable information, then check out 'Bringing Human Back'! The book is full of brilliant practical advice to help business owners at any stage of their journey, and I love how the author has not only drawn on her own life experiences, but on previous client experiences too. As someone who has struggled with motivation personally, the book not only gave me the tools I needed to confront my issues but gave me the ability to learn and develop from them. Most importantly, it made me realise I don't have to beat myself up about business all the time, we're only human! The author is a total straight-talking ball-buster and super funny too which makes for an awesome read – One to keep close and refer back to! Thank you SJ." *L-B Smith, Bespoke Mural*

"This book is very real and relatable, the author lays bare her life experiences and why she does what she does, it's like she's right there next to you, guiding you through the trials and difficulties of setting up your own business, and making that leap. Highly recommend." *S Fell*

Bringing Human Back

How to be more
successful in
business by
being you

Sarah-Jane Adams

ISBN 978-1-5272-7669-7

Cover design by Natalie Gladstone Design
www.nataliegladstonedesign.co.uk

Editing and typesetting by Fuzzy Flamingo
www.fuzzyflamingo.co.uk

Thank you to the people and the situations that have left me in a dark hole. So dark that all I could do was fight, fight my way back, learn, evolve and become a stronger version of me. You have made me who I am, and I am eternally grateful.

CONTENTS

About the author   ix
Acknowledgements   xi
Introduction   xiii
Believe in a solution without being
Blinded by the problem   xv

1. BE YOU DO YOU BE SUCCESSFUL AS YOU   1
   Underpinning the values of your business   3
2. FAILURE IS YOUR FRIEND   11
   Leave the negative connotations at the
   door, failure only exists if you let it   13
3. BUILDING SOLID FOUNDATIONS   21
   Brick by brick   23
4. DROP YOUR BALLS   29
   (Your metaphorical ones that is!)
   And stay in control   31
5. MEOW, MEOW AND MEOW SOME MORE   37
   Take the time to connect with others and be
   willing to adapt your approach   39
6. LISTEN   47
   Always listen   49
7. WHO WILL BUY YOU?   57
   Refining and defining your customer   59

8. PERFECT PACKAGING   65
   Keeping it simple   67
9. DON'T PULL YOUR OWN PANTS DOWN
ON PRICE   73
   (Too many people will try and
   do that for you)   75
10. YOUR BUSINESS IS NOT A CHARITY AND
YOU ARE NOT A VOLUNTEER   81
   Making sense of it all   83
11. BELIEVE AND YOU WILL ACHIEVE   89
   Give yourself permission to believe
   in your business   91
12. THE STRUGGLE IS HARD,
KEEP ON HUSTLING   97
   "Everything will be OK in the end. If it's not OK
   it's not the end." J. Lennon   99
13. BE KIND TO YOURSELF AND
THOSE AROUND YOU   105
   "Every day may not be good but there
   is good in everyday" – Unknown   107
14. THE SMALLEST STEPS MAKE THE
BIGGEST DIFFERENCE   113
   Never forget how far you have come   115
15. YOU ARE THE DIFFERENCE   121
   Your business on your terms   123
16. WHAT DOES SUCCESS LOOK
LIKE TO YOU?   129
   Know it and be true to it   131

CONTACT ME   137

ABOUT SARAH-JANE ADAMS

Sarah-Jane is a business mentor and coach. Involved in her family furniture business from an early age, she studied business and marketing at the University of Central Lancashire before forging a successful thirteen-year career in the corporate world in business strategy and development.

Driven by a desire to help individuals work more strategically, Sarah-Jane started Meow Consulting in 2018. Her mission is to help create the next generation of business leaders who forge new ways of working through simplicity, honesty and trust. Sarah-Jane is determined, knowledgeable and refreshingly honest. When not working, she can be found singing silly songs to her young daughter, running through the forest or sharing a bottle of wine with friends.

ACKNOWLEDGEMENTS

I want to say thank you to my husband, who when I walked away from the city never once made me feel bad, never once pointed out that it left us in a pretty challenging place financially, but believed in me and my ability to make my business a success.

I want to thank my mum for her love, her support and unending supply of stew and dumplings. She is an inspiration and I am tremendously proud of her.

To my nan for always believing in me and making me feel invincible. Teaching me to tell it like it is but with love in my heart.

I want to send love to those who I am blessed to call friends and family – my cheerleaders. The straight-talking ones who buy me a bottle of wine when I need it or just provide an ear. You make life worth living at the roughest of times and just bloody fun for the rest.

I am keen to thank everyone who has been involved in writing this book. Those who have encouraged me and most importantly those who have allowed me to share snippets of their story. Massive shout out to Cassandra Farren for mentoring me throughout this process.

And a huge thank you to each and every one of my clients, who have trusted me with their baby – their business!

I love you all.

INTRODUCTION

What's up!

Are you feeling lost? Are you constantly surrounded by people and those you love, but you still feel alone? Do you wonder if there is more to life than the 'slog' of the daily grind as an employee (in a job that leaves you numb) – working for people who you don't respect, who don't listen and where you feel frustrated? Or have you thought 'fuck this for a bunch of coconuts', walked away from the nine to five BS and joined the exhilarating world that is being a business owner? OR have you done the walking away, done the setting up your own thing and now struggle to stand out, make a profit and (God forbid) to actually enjoy what you are doing with your new-found freedom?

Well, if one of those is you, then this book is for you, my friend. I've done the trying to convince myself that the nine to five slog is the only way, I've done the 'just focus on the money', I've done the being propelled into a dark place, I've done the 'do you know what, there is more to life than this shit', I've done the 'fuck it, what is the worst that can happen?' I've done the 'this is scary but exhilarating', I've done the 'how the hell am I going to make myself heard, listened to and bought into?'. I've done this and I've got this – I've got you.

A word of warning...

Don't expect fluffy, templated bullshit. This book is real talk, real life and will enable real change. But please, please expect a shift in perspective (dare I say mindset!), anticipate changes that will make a direct positive impact on you, your life and your business. This book is about you taking a long look in the mirror, accepting change must happen (wherever you may be) and having the guts to be true to yourself.

It is about taking away the power of others who may doubt you, the naysayers, the haters, by not giving a damn what they think. Their opinions are a reflection of their own insecurities, their own limitations – so don't let them become yours. It is about feeling assured in your ability as a professional, as a human being. It is knowing that no one sees the struggles (of which there will be many) but just the success. It is about you knowing that the struggles are necessary for success to follow. It is about remembering the human behind your business – you. It is about remembering that your clients are also human. It is about being kind to yourself.

So... are you ready?

BELIEVE IN A SOLUTION WITHOUT BEING BLINDED BY THE PROBLEM

Where it all began

I sat on my sofa in the darkness of a November day, wrapped in the comfort of a dressing gown and my head shrouded in an oversized woolly hat, as tears rolled down my face. I felt defeated, humiliated and utterly incapable. I had handed in my notice a few weeks earlier and, after the sheer relief had passed, I was clinging to the edge of a cliff. I walked calmly into a meeting room, broke down in tears as I called my mum and said I needed to see the doctor. I was signed off work immediately. Getting out of there was a wonderful relief, but also an admission that I was beaten. Running over scenarios in my head of what I could have done differently, better – walked away with my head held high rather than hidden under a hat. They say the strongest fall the hardest and I most definitely had suffered a bloody huge blow. I could only see darkness, there was no glimmer of light. Everything was black and I was petrified. I felt so alone it was impossible to articulate. I was surrounded by so many people that cared but it was only me in my mind. I felt hopeless. I felt alone. I felt afraid. I saw no point in life and, to be honest, I saw no future.

Chaos

I had been working at an international professional services firm, working in a chaotic and negative environment – there was no satisfaction and there was no joy. As someone who always believed in what they brought to the table, I felt as though I was operating with both hands tied behind my back. My contribution had been watered down and I felt demotivated. I had never wanted to get up and walk out of a job, until then. The heart palpitations I had felt every evening since the day I began were ignored. It was only when my body and mind shut itself down that I realised how much it had affected me.

Propelled from darkness

I knew my loved ones were worried, really worried. I knew they didn't recognise me; fuck, I didn't recognise myself. A client and friend, Dee Anderson, said eloquently a long time after this that it is when we are backed in to a corner that we learn the most. My God was she right. I didn't know it then, but I know now that I needed to be in this place, however dark, to learn and to be propelled to a place where I was always meant to be. It did take me a while of feeling lost in that thick wood to dare to squint upwards and see a way forward. It was a place I do not want to ever return to, but a place that gave me the courage and strength to think 'fuck it' I am going to do this. By 'this', I mean set up my own business.

The rebuild

I fought so bloody hard to build myself back up. I had counselling, took time for me, refused medication, exercised and was patient with myself. For someone with a frenetic mind this was a massive challenge. I will never forget the counsellor saying, 'You will have many negative thoughts that come into your mind but that does not mean you have to engage with them. Let them pass.' Advice I repeat to myself and others often. If it doesn't bring something positive, tell it to jog on. When I look back now, I am proud that I was able to keep my big girl panties on even though the elastic threatened to snap at any moment, I am proud of myself for believing in me, I am proud because I may have broken down but I was not going to accept I was broken.

Flipping it

I flipped what was a real shitter of a situation. I chose to learn from it, I chose to think what is this trying to teach me and how can I use it to get where I need to be? I chose to look for the positive and I found it. I refused to harbour ill-feeling to the individuals who had left me without identity and value, and thanked them for forcing me to make that change. I realised that they only had control over how they made me feel if I let them. I was resentful of being put on my arse for a variety of reasons – it made money a real worry, it made starting a family impossible – but I chose to use it to question silly concerns, to change long-held beliefs. Am I beginning to sound like a self-help book? I hope not, I am not qualified. I suppose, in short, I realised I had a choice. A choice to focus on the good rather than the bad. And when I made that commitment to myself, I never looked back.

Not just talking the talk

From somewhere, I found the strength to get the ball rolling and began setting up my new business. I spoke to those who had trod that path before me, gained valuable insights and went for it. How many times had I shared a glass of wine with a buddy, consoling each other about having to accept the daily slog of life? Well, not anymore! Things were going to change, and I was going to make damn sure they did! As I sit here now nearly three years on, I am beaming from what I have created, beaming for what I have achieved, beaming because I was not willing to accept the drudgery and I now have a life that is anything but dull. I love what I do, I love how I help clients* and I love who I work with.

My mum commented about a year in, 'So, are you actually making any money? Because you never talk about money anymore.' This highlighted two key things: historically I only got joy from what I earned (not the actual job) and I now had so much more to be joyous about. For the record, I recall my first end of year meeting with my accountant. He sat smiling at me, saying what a spectacular first year I'd had – that he never sees this in a business that starts from nothing and I'd earned twice what he expected. My business continues to thrive.

> **Lesson:** Just because money isn't your reason for getting out of bed in the morning, doesn't mean you won't earn it.

The sad truth

My friends, there will always be challenges, problems, barriers that try and stop you from getting where you want to be but choose to ignore them. Because I can bet you anything that if that is all you focus on, then that is all you will see. However, if you make the choice to seek out the solution – you may not always know it and have to ask for help – you will find one. If you believe it exists you will work out how to make it work for you.

Make that choice

We have all had a real pisser of a day, where every damn thing has gone wrong. Where we drag ourselves home with the royal hump and then something happens. The smallest of things, but it makes us smile and snap out of our mood. I ask, why would you choose to go back to being miserable when you can focus on the good (however seemingly small and insignificant)? Because

I can guarantee you will feel far better for letting the crappy happenings of the day go. You will be a nicer person to be around, make more rational decisions and feel more in control.

Seeing the light

We have all been there, stuck in the thick wood having lost the capability of seeing the trees. We feel stuck, cornered, and all we can see are barriers. We feel overwhelmed and plain lost. The more we focus on the problems we perceive we face the more we see. Thick in the fog of problems we do not see the glimmer of light. There is always a glimmer of light, it is just a matter of choosing to look for it.

Bringing this mindset to business

Whether you are on the verge of starting, have launched recently or are an old hat in owning a business, this is a vital lesson. Vital because the challenges will be far more than you ever imagined. So, if you are serious about it, and I mean really serious – then give yourself the best chance. Believe you will overcome all the shit-covered balls that are catapulted your way, will find a way through and don't get lost in a fog of 'I can't do this'.

Food for thought

Time to find that mirror – think about a time you approached something with confidence, unwilling to be defeated. How did it feel? What was the end result? Now think of a time you went in to a situation already feeling defeated. What was the end result on this occasion?

If you are honest, I would guess that in the first situation you came out on top, smiling from ear to ear – whilst the second, you were pissed off and got nowhere. It is a choice. Moving forward is a choice.

Over to you: So... are you ready? The book can be spliced into three sections:

1. Foundations – being clear on the what, why, who and how
2. Framework to your ideas - a plan for the business to hang on and
3. Focus on you – the person behind the business.

It will challenge you as a business owner, it will challenge how you think and it will challenge how you approach your business. I can and will help you to make a change but it is you, and only you, who has the responsibility to see it through – to make it happen. This will have to come from you, do you have the minerals? Change is scary but it can also be really exhilarating. Are you ready to don your captain's hat? As guess what, you are the one steering your path forth. I say to all of my clients: the time has to be right for you and no-one can determine when that is apart from you.

Be prepared to do some reflecting, some thinking on the past, the now and the future while reading this book. Whether you are a thinker and process it mentally, get ready to start firing up that internal dialogue or if you have to get it out on paper, then keep a notebook and pen to hand!

Are you aching to take back control, see things in a new light, be so excited you can't sleep, have to pinch yourself daily as you can't possibly enjoy work this much...? Then grab that fucking hat and read on.

Let's do this!

SJ x

* For the record, I will interchange between using client, customer, buyer etc. we all use different terms. Ultimately, they mean the same.

1

BE YOU
DO YOU
BE SUCCESSFUL AS YOU

UNDERPINNING THE VALUES OF YOUR BUSINESS

The cold bucket of water in the face moment

Have you ever had a moment when you realised that there are loads of other people doing what you do? How the hell do you stand out? Why on earth is anyone going to listen to you when there are others who have been doing the same thing for nearly a decade longer? How can you make your offering different when ultimately it is the same? How do you foster the confidence to believe you do it better? And, how can you communicate this to your potential clients / customers / buyers / referrers / suppliers?

Sense check

When I first heard someone say, 'Listen, if you have plenty of competitors that is a good thing' I was confused – how could this be? It means you have more people to fight to get the work, no? When they pointed out that it actually verified the reason and need for your product or service, I got it. If you are lucky enough to have thought or discovered an untapped offering, great! But the majority of us don't work that way.

Giving your business the space it needs to evolve

When working with my clients I always encourage them to kick-off with an 'underpinning the values of the business' session. Why? To crystalise why they are different and because this is what gives them the freedom to explore and adapt how they work now and in the future. Ultimately, we don't recognise our individuality – the elements that make us different from the rest. These elements are what differentiates us from our competitors. And, there is *always* a difference. By uncovering the personal values of the business owner and combining these with their business values it determines how the business works, who they work with and how they work with them. Without these weighty pegs, your business could well blow away! Cut adrift with no direction.

When you set up you want and need control over what you offer and how you work. This control can sometimes tip in to a fear. A fear of changing, adapting how you work and innovating depending on the changing external environment in which you operate. We live in a fast-moving world, where the savvy consumer has high expectations and we must make damn sure we don't get left behind.

Lesson: Those that don't listen and adapt will be left behind. We must as business owners be willing and able to flex our approach depending on who we want to buy us and why. Things change and so must we. The beauty of getting to grips with our pegs (aka our values) means we can be safe in the knowledge that, however we evolve, we will always be true to what means most to us. Think of these values as our sounding board, that we check in with every so often, to ensure we are happy with how our business runs.

Know this and know it well

First rule of business: Accept you aren't going to be everyone's cup of tea.
Second rule of business: Accept you aren't going to be everyone's cup of tea.
Third rule of business: Accept you aren't going to be everyone's cup of tea!

Are you listening and taking this in? Don't waste time and energy chasing the wrong people.

Square peg, round hole

All too often I speak to business owners who don't recognise how they work and don't enjoy who they work with. They are forcibly stuffing how they work in to a hole they were never interested in, yet they hadn't even noticed. Two things: being clear on your values and who

your client is, is paramount. We will discuss this further
later on when we look at how we price what we do, but
when we accept not everyone is going to want to buy
us, things will become far easier and clearer. Don't take
it personally because this is business.

Over to you: Grab a big piece of paper and a pen (or a
pencil if you are like me). Draw a line down the centre
and write 'Personal' one side and 'Professional' the
other. Take some time to evaluate what is important
to you personally, what attributes do you hold dear –
for me straight-talking honesty and being respectful
of others have been what I have made every effort to
be and what I expect from those I work and play with.
Write down the qualities that resonate most with
you, these do not have to mean or be understood by
anyone else. Now move to the other half of the page.
List all of your previous roles, don't miss out any! I say
this because of the number of times a client has said
'oh, that role has had no bearing on what I am doing
now' and, in fact, it was the role that was pivotal to
bringing a key skill to the fore. I'll give you an example:
a very successful financial adviser questioned noting
down a previous job as a hairdresser – but it was
this very role that enabled them to hone the skill of
connecting with people from all walks of life. A skill
that was key to success in their business and one
that set them apart from the rest of their profession.

Now consider, what aspects of each role did you enjoy and what did you detest. How did each align with the most important attributes you noted? Tie in what is important to you personally with what you enjoy doing – this will shape how you want to work and highlight your values behind your business! I mentioned honesty and respect were two of my key qualities – I looked at roles where I felt I was most able to work in this way, with others who observed the same way of working. This is now fundamental to how I work with not only each client but all who I come into contact with – personally and professionally. This fusion of attribute and skillset is going to be different for everyone and will be what makes you and your approach different.

Authenticity equals integrity

People buy from people, so always be you. Yes, it may sound cheesy sales patter but it is so true. I want to ask you, when was the last time you bought from someone you didn't like? And if you did, because the deal was too good to miss, would you return or recommend them?

Another reason (if we needed one!) to take the time to pinpoint our values – reminding ourselves means we will be consistent with how we work with our clients, how we talk to them, how we show we understand them, how we make them feel. We all want to know what we are going to get; consistency gives us comfort and proves the sincerity of the provider. These all build trust and we all know what follows when we trust or are trusted – we are recommended, and we get repeat business.

Be authentic. Be consistent. Be you.

Moment of realisation

I had a client recently break down in tears when I gently questioned why more of their business was not focused on an area they loved, a skill that gave them deep joy, a skill that was the reason they had found themselves within their industry for so many years and a skill that made them stand out from the rest. They had become lost in trying to be all things to all people, they didn't enjoy working on the majority of the projects they had won and they weren't earning what they deserved. This realisation occurred during our session and was the reason for the tears that followed. The shift in them after acknowledgeing and acting on this was dramatic – their energy returned, their confidence overflowed, their earning potential rocketed, and they felt in control of their business and its future.

Over to you: Making this shift first requires you to be ready to hear what you have been missing or plain ignoring. Are you ready? Okay, let every fear, concern and hang-up go. Ask yourself what makes you happy. What makes you tingle with excitement? What makes your heart sing with joy at the prospect of undertaking it? Is this joy-inducing product or service a big part of your business? If it isn't, then make it one. You owe it to yourself. The courage it took to go and do your own thing was immeasurable. Make it count by doing what makes you happy – when you love what you do it shows. And when it shows, people want your help! And when people want your help, you earn money!

Lesson: Give yourself the permission to do what you love, no not every aspect of running your business may make your heart sing – let's be realistic now – but if you feel like you are pushing water uphill all the time, what is the point? Why did you take the leap to go out alone? You may as well still be employed and being dictated to! Do what you want, how you want, with whom you want.

Food for thought

Remember you are an expert in your own area of experience. We have all encountered wallies, with no real-life experience, who get on their platform and spout complete shite. Don't be too scared to grab your own platform to share your great experience and ideas. Remember to do this with confidence, with pride and with kindness.

Lesson: You don't have to be an arsehole in business to be successful. Always be kind, it will be repaid in abundance in the future. BE YOU. DO YOU. BE SUCCESSFUL AS YOU. "Always remember you are braver than you believe, stronger than you seem and smarter than you think." Winnie the Pooh.

2

FAILURE IS YOUR FRIEND

LEAVE THE NEGATIVE CONNOTATIONS AT THE DOOR, FAILURE ONLY EXISTS IF YOU LET IT

Rabbit in headlights

Have you ever been paralysed by fear? Fear of not achieving what you in a moment of madness believe you can. Fear of not reaching the heady heights of what others may expect of you. Fearful that if you pop your head above the parapet and fall flat on your face you will be deafened by 'I told you so's'. Fearful that you will accomplish nothing and fail.

Failure – what does it mean to you?

It's what most of us say is what stops us from doing things – or the fear of failure does at least. This fear is an interesting one to unpick and interesting because nearly every time, this incapacitating emotion is unfounded. I have understood failure to be many things over the years, letting yourself down, letting others down, not comparing to others as you think you should, things not going to plan, things not panning out as others planned.

What have I realised?

That any expectation we put upon ourselves from others is meaningless – often the others in question have no idea you have placed such weight on their opinion, they may not even be aware of what you are doing altogether. What a bloody waste of your emotion. Alternatively, when it comes to how we perceive ourselves, we can fall into that trap of making a comparison, a comparison that is frankly like comparing an apple to an orange – they both may be fruit and grow on a tree but that is where the similarity ends. So why do we persist on doing this with our peers? Another total waste. Don't do it, never do it and ignore those that encourage you to do it. So, I ask you again, what does failure mean to you?

If we learn, then we can never fail

Speak to the most 'successful' people (we will come back to what success means to us later on) and you will hear them utter that failure does not exist. And I for one believe them. They talk of failure being a liar, being something that is fabricated by those who themselves are too fearful to put themselves out there and so make up rubbish to stop others doing what they could not.

What does failure mean?

Well, that you tried something, and it didn't turn out like you had hoped or expected. What must we take from this? Two things: firstly, that we tried for a start, never overlook the courage that it took, and secondly that we were afforded the opportunity to learn something new. Two massive positives in my mind! We can look to Nelson Mandela for further proof of this myth around the existence of failure. *"Do not judge me by my successes, judge me by how many times I fell down and got back up again."* I don't see any mention of the word failure here – of which, by many, there would have been countless. When a child first tries to walk and falls, do they give up? Are they branded a failure? No! They are encouraged to keep trying and learning as only then will they master what they wish to achieve.

Lesson: Not trying is failing. For me the fear of setting up my own business and it going tits up was only outweighed by the fear of not trying at all. I realised this would have been one of my greatest regrets. So, when I stop trying – no matter how many fantastic fuck ups I make (of which there will be lots), then that will be the day I know it is time to do something new.

Fall in love with failure

'Failure' is your friend. Let us take the time to look at failure and what it means in another way, from another perspective. Something positive from all the negative guff that normally surrounds it, engulfs it.

FAILURE shows you are trying, and I mean really trying.
FAILURE means you are not afraid of pushing the boundaries.
FAILURE means you are not only learning new things but new ways to do things.
FAILURE proves you won't be put off by bumps in the road.
FAILURE is something that happens when you are courageous.
FAILURE is your friend, it teaches you so much, nurtures your talent and drives you to achieve big things.

Failure is getting back up time and again and being that much stronger every time.

Over to you: I want you to think of a time something didn't go to plan. Think of a time that the shit really hit the fan. What happened? How did you react? What was the outcome?

A real-life example: I recall back in the day, when I was a junior at a recruitment advertising agency working for a well-known global charity. I made the cardinal sin of getting the salary wrong on the printed advert, bear in mind that we were spending large sums on advertising for a charity that had to be exact in their investment. It was a massive oversight on my part and 100% should not have happened. What did I do? I called the newspaper, explained my error and managed to get it changed on some editions (it was global, so had different print deadlines for different countries). I made an immediate change to the online version. I called not only the manager I was reporting to at said charity but also his big boss. What was the outcome? Okay, so my boss was pissed off, but could not fault my 'hands up' approach with the client. I did not try to skirt responsibility. The big boss at the charity may have spoken to me a handful of times but now knew me, and not just for the fuck up but, because I was honest. The manager I was dealing with directly was thankful that he didn't have to break the news to his boss. They respected me for my honesty and our relationship thereafter was stronger because of it. I built better relationships at the newspaper so was able to negotiate better rates going forward and I changed internal processes to make sure it never happened again. So, a pretty toe-curling experience turned around. Did I fail or did I learn? I learned and I grew massively because of it. Had I hidden under my desk and denied all responsibility I would have learned and earned zip.

Lesson: It is *always* how we react to situations that means the most. We are human and we all make mistakes. Think of when you are in a restaurant and the food you can't wait to eat turns up cold. If you are like me, you can be pretty fierce when hangry! When the response from the staff is a grunt and you have to watch the rest of your table polish off their grub before yours makes a reappearance AND no discount is given off the bill, you are not happy, and you never go back. However, if the response is a sincere apology, the owner or the chef may even apologise – your food is prioritised in the kitchen meaning you get to eat with the rest of your party, and you are offered a free glass of wine while you wait – HAPPY DAYS! You remember the restaurant for their outstanding service rather than their error. Think about that next time you want to run and hide. Think about the lasting impression you want to create and what you want to be known for. This will always be more powerful than any 'failure'.

Food for thought

I want to leave you with a quote from Goodrich: *"Many times what we perceive as an error or failure is actually a gift. And eventually, we find that lessons learned from that discouraging experience prove to be of great worth."*

If it wasn't already obvious, I don't believe in failing, 'failing' is such a negative connotation for something that represents something so positive. When we switch our mindset on how we perceive failure and make it something encouraging and constructive, we find the fear that often comes with it melts away. Next time you approach something that scares you, take away the power the fear of failing brings, embrace it and see it as something to learn from which will set you in better stead in the future.

3

BUILDING SOLID FOUNDATIONS

BRICK BY BRICK

Leap of faith

Okay, so you have, or are imminently, going to jump out of the safe employed nest into the unknown. You have decided to make the leap because you have a technical skill that is way too remarkable for someone else to be profiting from more than you. OR you are bursting with a passion that drives you eagerly forward to change the game. OR you are pushed into doing something you have always dreamed of. How do you feel when you leap? What happens next? Do you tumble downwards and see where you land, or do you look at this exciting new expanse of possibility and then plan your descent? You may feel overwhelmed by the decision and those big pants you pulled on in order to make it are weighing you down. You feel yourself tumbling and hoping for the best.

STOP!

Fight that downward force. You must recognise that you need to logically think this through – the business you plan to build will not be built by you tumbling but by you placing strong foundations, brick by brick.

Build, build and build some more

Let me use an example to not only bring this one to life a bit but to showcase the importance of this foundation building, and what we are risking if we don't factor this in early on. Imagine you are having an extension on your house: arguably the most essential element when building a house are the foundations, this is also true for business. You are making the living space larger with a cracking new kitchen. It is a big investment, with a lot at stake – your home and probably the majority of your savings! If you are honest, you aren't much (well most of us might not be) interested in the complex engineering aspects of the foundations, you are just chomping at the bit to start making this beautiful new space look great and feel like home. As you see the budget sprint away, you realise you may have to rethink the choice of kitchen and appliances to ensure all the essential work is carried out to underpin the footings of this new build.

QUESTION: You would never forgo investing in important foundation work to keep that kitchen dream alive, would you? You know the whole build would collapse. So why would we do the same with our business?

Applying the same techniques, levelling the ground by understanding your 'why', adding in the sand and clay with your values (as we spoke about in chapter 1) and then reinforcing it with the cement by being really clear about who you are targeting, with what and how you are going to reach them. The steel beams will be the financials, you know, the calculations around money that you may be avoiding – breaking down what you offer, understanding your profit margins, carefully selecting your suppliers, working out your pricing – knowing what you are going to earn! Are you still with me? It can be easy, too easy, to get lost in the momentum, the excitement and not give yourself the time to do this. You may be fine for a while, but it will catch up, you may plateau, you may suffer losses, you may lose direction. Put the graft in early and avoid this, it is unnecessary and can be incredibly damaging to both you and your business. So, don't get lost in the pretty stuff (what I was referring to in the guise of the kitchen) like spending ages on designing a logo, or a new website before you work on the nitty gritty. That pretty stuff will be far more powerful if it is well considered and is promoting a robust business.

Breaking it all down in order to rebuild it stronger

A real-life example: Have you ever worked at something and struggled to get anywhere? Your desire is strong, and you've invested the time in trying to improve but you are not making those expected leaps forward? I was reminded of my own advice while swimming recently, you see I have been learning front crawl for a while, it is so hard! Swimming is one of those sports that you can't just go ahead and do – like running – without knowing some techniques, however limited. Much like business.

Anyway, back to the swimming – give me breaststroke and I can swim 3km, but front crawl and 50 metres would kill me. Good news! I had a breakthrough. Instead of trying to haphazardly mash together the intricacies of the stroke and panicking about doing them, I took my approach back to basics. I took time to focus on each movement, really think how they all came together, I slowed it down. And it worked!! I broke all the individual elements down, so I could rebuild them in a more effective and, dare I say, successful way. The result, I went from a 'hope for the best' 50m to a fluid 600m.

My point here is that I had to strip it back in my own way to make it work for me. It felt like taking two steps backwards but in doing so, I ultimately propelled myself forwards. Stopping to do the foundation work can feel a bit frustrating, like you are covering old and known ground, and it is a waste of time. BUT it is an incorrect assumption. Give yourself the permission to do a bit of back-peddling and side-peddling (does that exist?) and I promise it will set you in much better stead. You will always learn and you will most certainly see bigger strides in success.

Over to you: We all need a guide. Some tips on where to begin.

- **Plan** what you want to do with your business, where you want to be in the next year, three years, five years and more.

- **Make yourself accountable by setting goals** and always remember to pat yourself on the back when you achieve the smallest of milestone.
- **Breakdown each product or service** you offer.
- **Understand profit margins** for each of the above.
- **REMEMBER**: your strategy should both support and be consistent with your vision.

Lesson: Laying proper foundations for our business is intrinsically linked with plotting our journey ahead – the structure of our business. Do not learn the hard way and risk becoming lost and disheartened. We wouldn't travel somewhere new without checking out a map, would we? We would inform ourselves of the directions and how we are going to get there. Don't go into business without a map, and definitely don't forget to use it. We are responsible for its success, we must nurture and love it. Another reminder of the importance of working on the business instead of just in it. Taking that step back and looking at our businesses objectively can be really hard, sometimes we need help. If you need that help, invest in it. You are ultimately investing in your future.

Food for thought

A short and sweet parting thought from me on this subject, after many a conversation with clients about why they needed to get their map and pen out. Laying those foundations means we are forced to identify our future, our plans and where we want to reach.

If we don't know where we are going, how will we know when we get there?

DROP YOUR BALLS

4

(YOUR METAPHORICAL ONES THAT IS!) AND STAY IN CONTROL

How long have you been juggling?

Are you too busy to stop, but too busy to carry on? Those bloody balls must be breeding because they are multiplying by the day, right? You know you have to do something, but one false move and those buggers will all come tumbling down and you will never be able to pick them all up again. You are not in a circus, although you may feel like it, it is time to stop the pretence and well, just stop. It is time to put those balls down. It is time to allow yourself to get some perspective. It is time to get more clarity on what you are working on, what you should be working on and what you must work on. It is time to take back control.

Put those balls down

Clarity comes when we stop and put those balls down. Without clarity, we cannot truly be in control and, when we are out of control, we make bad decisions. And let's get this straight – clarity is not something other people have, and you do not. It is not jargonistic bullshit.

It is there for the taking, by all of us! Give yourself the permission to press that pause button, take a breath and reorder those balls. At the risk of over-complicating this we also need to recognise that these balls come in different types – the day-to-day ones, the strategic ones, the admin ones, the opportunity ones. We'll leave the personal ones for the time being. Let's try and break this down.

A clean slate

So, the balls have finally been put down (what a relief!) – what do you find? Our day-to-day balls: there are the ones that you have been carting around that serve no purpose, the ones that have clones, the ones whose existence is questionable, the ones that are really important but can wait, and the ones that are really bloody urgent and need your immediate attention. Congratulations, you now have a to-do list. The beauty about tackling our day-to-day balls first is that it provides direction for the business in the short-term and this provides a foundation for all of our other balls. To complete our newly created to-do list, our admin balls will need to be parachuted in. All those lofty strategic balls, you know the ones – the neatly carved sections of your business that give you direction and focus – will drive the opportunity balls you take up. Are you still there or have I lost you? If you are beginning to glaze over, just tend to the day-to-day balls, then re-read this again!

Over to you: So how can you drop the balls and give your poor arms a rest? Do you need to take some time out? It may feel indulgent but stopping and getting yourself in order is absolutely vital. Do you need to outsource some of the tasks that are bogging you down? Yes, this can feel scary handing some of the control over but believe me when I say that other people can take care of your balls too!

A real-life example: I recall when working within my last place of employment feeling totally overwhelmed. I had so many different projects on and my usual control and sharp awareness of what needed to be done, by whom and by when, had long deserted me. I knew I had to take stock but the thought of taking time out to do so made me feel sick – I was drowning. I was just about to go on my honeymoon, so with the handover looming I was forced to do what I had been putting off – get my balls in order. It took two hours, I had over twenty projects running simultaneously, all at varying stages and each involving different members of the team. I created folders for each and labelled them. I collated all the paperwork in order and wrote a brief synopsis of where each project was, what action had to be taken and what the deadline was on a post-it note on the front of each (I even have pictorial evidence!). I ordered them on my desk, sat down and thought no wonder I've been so fucking frantic! Yes, it had taken two hours of precious time but wow it felt good. After grabbing a strong coffee, I felt like I was back in the game and on top of things once again. I was clearer on my instruction to others and was now able to confidently respond when questioned. I was back in control and others noticed. I did give myself a little kick in the shin for not doing it sooner and promised myself I would not get in to that position again. Don't get me wrong, the shit still hits the fan, I still have moments when the number of balls gets too great, but now I don't delay the 'big put down', so please don't you either. You may not work like me, so whatever works for you, but take that time to reflect and achieve some order!

Lesson: I've spoken to so many business owners who are just struggling with the amount of balls they are juggling. They know what they want to do and why they need to do it but have no idea how to press pause and start to take control. When you feel out of control in your business, in your life, it can be pretty damn scary. Scary because you don't know what way to turn or who to turn to. We may not want to admit it to ourselves, let alone others, but it is very much there, and the truth is, once we put our hands up and say 'I need help', everything immediately gets better. To make well-judged, consistent and comprehensive decisions we need to have a firm grip on all aspects of our business. This is only possible when we have a clear oversight of the bigger picture. And then when we have resumed the much-needed control we are ready to grasp every opportunity that comes our way.

Food for thought

Without control there is no clarity. Without clarity there is a real risk of wasting time and money in the short-term but looking forward this could have an impact on the success and direction of the business as a whole. Take my advice, drop your balls and give you and your business every chance of success it deserves.

5

MEOW, MEOW AND
MEOW SOME MORE

TAKE THE TIME TO CONNECT WITH OTHERS AND BE WILLING TO ADAPT YOUR APPROACH

Bear with me, I have not gone mad and I am not just a crazy cat woman – although it has to be said they are a firm fixture in my life. I worked in the city in business development and various other marketing roles for over thirteen years. One thing I learned: we all like to stay safe in how we communicate. We communicate in our language. We want to position ourselves as the knowledgeable professional, and there is nothing wrong with that until you forget who you are talking to and for what reason. In my roles, I worked with those at the top of their game, who'd spent years learning their trade and who knew it inside out. Their knowledge became so ingrained that they could not recall a time when they did not know it. Why was this a problem? It was a problem because when trying to sell their product or service they forgot the person buying it did not know what they knew. We have all been blasted with jargon and acronyms and thought 'huh?'. If your potential client is confused, it's unlikely they'll become a paying client. So, keep this in mind as you read on. Think about who is buying you, and by 'you' I mean whatever you are selling, and why they need you.

Times have changed, are you being left behind?

The way we buy has changed drastically over the last decade. Accelerated by the all-knowing worldwide-web, we have all become savvy consumers. Pair that with our crazy lives, and we are time-poor. Ultimately, we want to know what we are buying, and the internet allows us to find this out quickly. We expect whoever we are buying from to not only understand our need for buying but also the challenge we are facing that has created this need. Long gone are the days when you could bombard and blind potential clients with complex terminology that only you understand. This was made very apparent within the accountancy and legal market. There once was a time when the profession could circulate a jargon-heavy overview of their services to prospective clients – the response was 'I don't know what you are talking about, that must mean you do, and I don't need to, so I would like to work with you.' So, I ask you again – how do you package what you do? Is it user-friendly? Does it make sense to your potential buyers? Or does it just make sense to you?

So why the Meow?

There is good reason why I called my business Meow Consulting. After I help my clients to establish a robust structure within their business, we talk language and how they communicate their offering. All the good stuff I have been talking about already. Our beloved domestic cats are pretty incredible, and what more can we expect from a species that has not only conquered almost every environment on our planet but managed not only to survive *but* thrive. Cats have lived for thousands of years alongside humans. People allowed cats to domesticate themselves, we did not domesticate cats.

Any cat lovers amongst you will agree that they always know how to get what they want and this is largely down to how they communicate with us. Our shrewd little companions realised early on that we don't communicate in body language like they ordinarily would but instead we make sounds at one another. So, they began to 'meow' to get our attention and to get what they wanted from their human slaves. If you have more than one feline in your home you will notice they do not meow to one another. Even if you aren't a feline-fan, how can you not think this is amazing? I think it is bloody fantastic and gives a clear lesson to us humans, especially when it comes to business! All businesses. I'm not suggesting that you start meowing in your meetings! But I promise that by adapting your language you will not only succeed but you will excel. I'll leave that one with you to ponder on.

Showing not telling

Let me be really clear on this as it is pretty simple. Most of us have many competitors, others who offer the same as what we do. So why do people choose to work with us? They choose to work with us not just because we offer them a solution but because we show them we understand their challenge, the one that has led them to need our services. To be understood is a basic human need, and this carries through to business and why we buy. Don't tell people you know what they need – show them! Give examples of how you have helped others. Better yet, let happy customers tell them how good you are! Show you understand, don't tell them. If we have had a shit day and are in need of a hug there would be little gained in someone pointing out to us that we'd had a shit day. What we would benefit from is them showing us they understood by giving us a big hug! A basic example but an apt one.

Why do we forget...

Clients are buying from us because they do not have our skills. They do not know what we know. What does this mean? They have no clue what is involved in what we offer – that includes the years it has taken for us to be able to offer it, what the process of completing the work may look like and what each party will have to provide in order to finish the job successfully. This is intrinsically linked with value, which I will discuss in future chapters. ALWAYS take the time to walk your client through the process, explain each stage and its accompanying timeline. We all want to know what we are paying for. This opens a dialogue in your relationship and will pay dividends going forward. Don't be afraid of patronising them; if they know certain aspects, they will tell you! For me, anything to do with work on my house means that I want to be told explicitly what the job involves, how the cost factors into this, what they need from me and what I can expect from them at the end of the job. Managing expectations works both ways and setting clear guidelines early on is a necessity.

Over to you: Get out that large piece of paper again and draw three vertical columns. Now give them individual headings of 'service or product', 'solution' and lastly 'challenge'. In the first column, list all the services or products you sell. You will probably find this is how you have been labelling them and trying to sell them to date. Then, I want you to think hard about what is the solution they are offering a potential customer – we buy a solution, remember! Then work your way through to the challenge. Take time thinking about what situation your potential customer could be in to need your help – there could be more than one challenge for each offering. What you will find is the 'service or product' you had initially labelled will no longer serve a purpose, apart from to you. What you will be selling going forward is a solution whilst showing you understand their need by talking through the challenge currently faced.

Lesson: My point here is to bring to life what you do and how you can help. To make it easy to understand for your potential client. I will give you an example. One of my clients is a patent attorney, one of their services is 'applying and securing patents' on behalf of their clients. With that service in mind we tackled the task above. What do they sell now? 'Protecting the asset that underpins your business'. Don't you think this is way more powerful? And when it comes to driving home our understanding of their situation and need for our service we talk about 'protecting their research and development investment'. Immediately our service is understood and our ability and experience is clear. Is this starting to make more sense? Speak in plain language, keep it short and keep it simple!

Food for thought

We could be selling the same thing, but to different people it offers a different solution, as they will have experienced a different challenge. With that in mind, depending on who we are selling to, we would be packaging our offering in a very different way – as the way we package it is dependent on the particular need of a potential buyer. An example: the service is getting a manicure, one individual has an important business meeting and they want to look smart, another has a wedding to attend and has no nail varnish at home to match their outfit. Same service, two different challenges, and thus two different ways to sell the service. Get it?

Make it easy for them to buy in to you and from you. There is no point having an offering that can help many, but few understand. Talk in their language. MEOW!

LISTEN

ALWAYS LISTEN

Use those ears

When was the last time you were having a conversation and you knew the person you were talking to was not listening? Can you recall when someone was trying to sell you something, even though you had explicitly told them you have no interest or need in what they were selling – like a dog with a bone they carry on trying to flog you their wares. How utterly frustrating, disheartening and, well, plain annoying. Those two things on the side of our heads are often under-used. Make sure you are using them to their full potential. Please.

Are you listening?

Are you listening when you have conversations, being present and picking up on those diamond-nuggets that will set you apart from the rest? Are you listening to those who offer a similar service and have trod the path before you? Are you listening to the driven fellow business owners you meet? Are you listening to those you plan to partner and collaborate with in the future? Are you listening to the responses of those you approach before you launch in to your all-singing, all-dancing pitch? Are you listening to clients you have worked with in the past and those you work with currently? Are you listening to truly understand or are you just eagerly awaiting your turn to speak?

Leave your ego at the door

There are very few of us that revel in trying to secure business. We want to get in, tell them how great we are, for them to agree and sign up, then get out. When you are self-employed, you are always 'on', you never know what could come out of the most obscure exchanges. It is for this reason our opportunities to talk about what we do can consist of us vomiting our polished elevator pitch without even stopping to take a breath, let alone listen to what the other person is saying. The whole reason behind this book is to make business more human, so get used to me harking back to it regularly! So, on that thought, none of us like being talked at. Especially when we feel it is a pre-prepared speech, that has been used on many before us and probably on many after us. Cue the toe-curling cringe.

How do we quickly make a huge change to these situations before we go full-pelt into our beautifully-curated bullshit? Stop. Ask them open questions, find out more about who they are, what they do, what they struggle with. The real art is being able to respond and adapt your offering to their *individual* needs. Trust that you know your client's challenges and trust that you or one of your contacts have the perfect solution. When you feel relaxed, they will feel relaxed. Trust and rapport will be built so much quicker when you don't sound like a robot! Try it. I dare you.

> **Over to you:** Try these three beauties to get you started:
>
> 1. Tell me why and how you started your business?
> 2. What gets you up in the morning?
> 3. What is your biggest challenge – the one that keeps you awake at night?

Don't just talk the talk

You've refined how you have more successful conversations but how does this affect the rest of your business? You have a super-sexy offering, no one can deny that there is a real need for it. You have done all your due-diligence – you have identified who your client is, you know what you want your service to look like and you're even all over the figures. You have a clear path, a robust business strategy and structure and you just know this is going to work. Your passion and sheer love for what you do and belief in how you can help drives you forward. Hustling harder than you ever thought possible, six months in you look at your bank balance and think – what the actual fuck have I been doing? You have made one fatal mistake. In your enthusiasm to help you have not listened, really listened. To clients who have not come back. To those you have approached and have not been successful.

I spoke in an earlier chapter about knowing and owning the values in your business, how this enables you to flex and adapt how you work. This is where it comes in really handy. Our fierce passion and skill are what drives us, our unfaltering belief in what we can offer, our knowing of how we can help our customers. So, is it any wonder we get a little prickly when a suggestion is made that we are possibly doing something wrong, that we need to change our approach?

You are not alone

Fear not, we have all been there. We instantly assume any type of feedback or advice is a negative and therefore a slight against not only our business but our personal expertise. We go on the defence and our ears close for business. As a person with good intentions who is really trying to help, how could anyone possibly suggest we are doing it wrong? In switching off, we miss the opportunity to learn, to grow and to improve. Yes, not all criticism is constructive and this has to be taken with a pinch of salt. What you will find is those who excel in business are always keen to know how they can improve. They listen. They listen to their peers, their clients, their competitors, their collaborators – they listen.

It is often the smallest of changes that can make the biggest of differences. Something that initially makes us question our business, can, in fact, be simply turned around. By homing in on those values you can be sure to be happy with what you are doing, by listening and adapting, your clients will be happy with what you are providing.

Lesson: We cannot dictate how people buy us, so never try. However well-meaning it might be. We humans hold our freewill dear and we like to feel in control.

Real life example: A client had a successful vegan food business; their sole aim was not only to make vegan food accessible to all but to also dispel any myths around it tasting less than delicious. The goal was to create a shift in the mindset of those who bought their produce. To convert them to liking vegan food. BUT even though they recognised the huge change this would mean to many of their customers, they overlooked this in the way they communicated their products. Instead, messaging was aimed at individuals who already loved vegan food. They forgot how they had felt, what they had thought, and how they had been convinced to try vegan products all that time ago. We discussed the importance of language in the previous chapter. So, what in fact they had inadvertently done was to alienate those very customers they were trying to reach. They forgot to listen to their own messages, they forgot to listen to how they were being received and they forgot to step back and listen to their customers. A huge oversight. One, thankfully, we corrected.

Another cracking example of how this works in practice: in the late 1960s, Rupert Murdoch bought the ailing *The Sun* newspaper from the Mirror Group. In twelve short months Murdoch took the newspaper from the brink of disaster to a number one seller. How? He made the correct decision to actually listen to what his reader would like to read, unlike other newspapers at the time who dictated what their readers should read. Turns out they wanted more sport and sex and that's what Murdoch gave his reader. *The Sun* excelled. Pretty impressive. And how? By listening! An intuitive yet simple move. A move that has seen *The Sun* stay at the top for decades – whether you are a reader or not, it's an approach to be noted.

Over to you: We recognise that there are dark arts that plant stealthy seeds, seeds that grow and cause a reaction. We feel like we own this reaction, that it was us who planted that seed, but we are wrong. We need to make sure we allow our potential buyers to continue to think this way. How can you plant seeds that flourish? Think about what you offer, how you work. Who have you spoken to in the last six months who didn't go ahead with your proposal? Don't be afraid to ask for advice, feedback and areas you could improve. It may feel like you are dropping your façade, but someone who cares will always win out against those who are too scared or arrogant to ask.

Food for thought

We have two ears and one mouth for a reason. Make the most of that extra appendage. Remember what we learn from listening might not necessarily have an instant impact, sometimes you need to bank these nuggets and whip them out at the most opportune time. Always think long-term in business. An obsession with quick-wins will set the ball rolling for an unstable future.

7

WHO WILL BUY YOU?

REFINING AND DEFINING YOUR CUSTOMER

You are gagging to get going but where do you begin? There are so many avenues you could pursue but which one do you choose first? Do you know who to approach? Do you know who would bite your hand off for your help? Do you know who would be best placed to help you connect with the right people? Do you really know where to begin?

Giving yourself the best opportunity

So, you've got a cracking idea. You know this is going to fly. But have you thought about who is going to buy it? May sound bloody obvious but it's not going to be everybody's bag and you need to know whose bag it is! Snap up the opportunity early on to get damn clear on who should be your prime targets. Make it easy for yourself. To coin a shocking corporate phrase – pick the low-hanging fruit (yuck!).

Don't try to push water uphill

Being clear and focused on who the hell you're trying to talk to will save you a lot of time, energy and money.

It will make the process of defining your ideal targets a whole lot easier. We all prefer to chunk things down and this will enable you to do just that. Yes, you will be able to help many different clients for different reasons but if you try and do it all at once you will make it more difficult than it needs to be. It will dilute your offering, your energy reserves and your ability to do the job to your best ability. You'll be growing multiple trees and be back in the "can't see the wood for the trees" place. Don't do it. Be clear. Be intent on who you want to talk to and know why they need you. Again, you're not going to be everyone's cup of tea (second reminder), so if you're not getting anywhere with someone you've thought was ideal, move on! It can be hugely demoralising and frustrating. Neither emotion will serve you well. Don't waste your time and energy. Energy is valuable, so don't fritter it away.

Over to you: It's that time again! Get your pen and paper out. Make two columns: one for those who would benefit from your offering, the other for those who wouldn't. It's often easier to start with who you can't or don't want to help. Write it down. We have already explored how we best sell our services in chapter five and now you can align and tweak these with specific targets in mind.

A real-life example: Whipping out that scattergun can seem like the only option. From working in the big corporates to fledgling start-up businesses I have seen it happen across the board. The desire and need to earn some money, whilst being faced with the challenge of not knowing where to begin, forces even the most sensible to target every man and his dog. Without really stopping to think if the dog is interested in their services, let alone needs them. I would be sleeping on a pretty penny if I had a pound for the times I've asked, 'So who are we trying to sell to here?' The response being a vacant expression, stuttering and a vague, pull-at-straws reply. When I push more, I see the little lightbulbs sparking to life above their heads, 'Oh, so that is why we didn't get the response we expected, because they actually aren't the right fit for us?' The relief floods off them in waves. It wasn't that they had a crap offering, it wasn't that their charisma had departed them, and it definitely wasn't that they weren't up to the job. They had simply approached the wrong person. Why? Because they hadn't put enough thought into who the right person was before they had made that call.

Competing for competing sake

I recall when working at an Accountancy firm, one of the most respected partners approached the business development team with an instruction to create and craft a new offering, to a new client base. The fact that our team didn't have accounting expertise or the manpower to actually do the job were ignored. The fact that the team were already drowning with work was ignored. The fact that taking on new work would compromise the quality of their service to their current clients was ignored. Whilst they recognised that they were busy, they became distracted and some might say greedy trying to compete with their competitors. It was a 'keeping up with the Jones's' pursuit that ultimately risked the morale of their team and the service received by existing, valuable clients. They went ahead despite our protestation and the shit hit the fan. Like a movie, everything we said would play out, did, and they had to make a U-turn, sharpish. Just focus on what you are good at, not what others are doing. Don't compete for the sake of it. Choose your battles.

Lesson: [If you are like me,] I believe I can help anyone, at any stage of their business and within any industry. This can sometimes make it tough to nail down who I'm chasing. Instead of focusing on the type of client, I focus on the situation they may be in that has led them to need my help. In doing that it allows me to be more focused around who I pursue. For example, those who may be struggling with pricing. This could be having a catastrophic effect on their profits and making them question the viability of their business. So, I focus on business owners faced with this specific challenge. Rather than trying to carve out a type of client, I concentrate on their challenge. Does this make sense? It is all about being more efficient and in order to be effective we must have a target in mind. Think about firing a bow and arrow, you know you've hit the target as there is only one to hit. If you had multiple targets, how on earth would you evaluate the success of your archery skills? And how would you know what target to focus on hitting first?

Food for thought

Breaking down your potential customers, understanding their drivers, and truly putting yourself in their shoes. It is not just identifying the need, it is understanding how you are going to cause them to act by pushing a trigger. Remember we talked about planting those stealthy seeds? Don't be afraid to leverage your network nor underestimate the power of asking for a happy client to refer you to their peers.

As the landscape in which you operate changes, so will your product or service. This too will mean that your ideal customer changes. Check back in every so often and ensure you're still knocking on the right doors. If you have refined and defined your ideal client, those doors will keep on opening!

PERFECT PACKAGING

8

KEEPING IT SIMPLE

You've worked out what you are selling and to who, so how do you make it irresistible?

The best things come in small packages

Don't be afraid to be really specific and niche about what you offer. We've all seen the explosion of burger-only restaurants. Why? Because it has allowed them to really nail their product, to make it the best it possibly can be and to not be distracted by other grub that would otherwise dilute the quality of their menu. We can all fall into the trap of trying to be 'all things to all people'. Why? To maximise our earning potential, to compete with a competitor's offering and to not put all our eggs in one basket. What we don't do is realise that we can't be shit-hot at everything and so we weaken our offering. Like the best business owners that don't pretend they can do everything within their business – be the accountant, the social media expert, the strategist, etc., etc. – do not feel like you have to offer and be good at everything. The quality is harder to maintain and that consistency we strive for can be quickly lost. Our potential customers are so confused by what we do actually offer, they buy

nothing at all. Keep it simple. Keep it clear. Keep it easy
to buy.

Make it simple

Whatever you are selling and whoever you are selling it
to, they want it to be easy. Easy to understand, easy to
purchase and easy to solve their problem. Packaging our
products or services in the right way means it forces us
as business owners to be clear about where our offering
begins and ends BUT it also makes it totally clear to
the buyer what they are getting. We've discussed the
importance of managing expectations in an earlier chapter.

A real-life example: The mighty meal deal! Whether in
Tesco, McDonald's or any number of eateries (are you
starting to see a theme with me using food examples, can
you tell I like my grub?), how successful has this been?
What has it offered? A simple idea – you know what you
are getting and for what price and we can't get enough of
them! It has enabled businesses to bring together many
different products and allows the customer the control
over how to match them. The best of both worlds and this
takes me neatly on to a further point. Putting a structure
around what you offer does not mean the customer
loses their ability to cherry-pick what is best for them.

Organised fun

Does it exist? Of course it does! Much the same as being
able to mould your offering around an individual client's

needs without losing control of how you work. Putting in the leg-work so you know what works for you as a business owner is key – I'm thinking profit margins, ability and desire to do the job, time constraints, etc. This allows you to break down each aspect and then draw them back together in different ways to not only suit you but ultimately your client too. Whilst I have spoken about not dictating how we are bought, we do need to set a precedent around how we can be bought. Having something under control makes it easier to manage those all-important expectations, for both parties, and makes for a far more fluid way of working. Think of a maze: there is a start and an end point. But there are different ways of getting to that end point. Navigate your client through that maze in a way that both makes sense and suits them.

Suck it and see

But in an ideal world this of course cannot always be possible. If you have just started your business and are doing the wise thing of trialling what you do and how you do it, OR, if you have recently launched a new offering, it is always about learning as you go. Because, after all, trying new things is hugely positive for you, your business and your customers. As long as you stop to learn and reflect, it will allow you to neatly bag these little gems.

> **Lesson:** Have you ever felt restricted in what you can buy and it has led you not to buy at all? Equally have

you felt like you needed guidance from the 'expert' you have approached and yet they have left it up to you to work it all out. Working out that middle ground can be tough for us business owners. Think back to that maze analogy. Structure your offering around this concept. Give your potential buyer a start point: their current situation and challenge. Get clear on what they need from you: the finish point. Now walk them through their options and how they could get there. Got it?

Over to you: Whatever you offer, there will be distinct elements that are interdependent. Carve them up. Do your due diligence and work out the numbers, the time, the external parties needed to offer each. Consider how your products or services have been bought previously. Now using the knowledge of the past buyer behaviour, begin to bundle them together. These often naturally fall into different categories, determined by different budgets. Creating your bronze, silver, gold and even platinum packages. A word to the wise, don't name your packages something that could be seen as unfavourable, like 'the basic package'; when we are investing in something, we don't want to feel that investment is being sneered at as the cheapest option. Simply by changing it to 'the foundation package' it immediately shifts the perception. Back to the neat bundles... so you now have some digestible ways to sell your wares. If you do have any super special extras, these can be flagged and costed as add-ons. They will be easier for you to sell and easier to be bought.

Food for thought

Package what you do, how you would like to buy it. Remind yourself how you buy and why.

9

DON'T PULL YOUR OWN PANTS DOWN ON PRICE

(TOO MANY PEOPLE WILL TRY AND DO THAT FOR YOU)

Okay, so I may seem to be being flippant, but I am as serious as hell when it comes to this. Can I ask how you place value on something? What does the price of something say about its perceived quality?

What does the steadfast belief of the seller in both their offering and the accompanying price tag say to you? What does it tell you about them as a business? What does it tell you about their offering? What does it say about the quality? In turn, how does that make you equate the price with the quality of the offering?

Valuing what you do, starts with you

How you perceive your value is ultimately how others will perceive it. Don't underplay the years of toil you invested to reach where you are or the precious time your client has with you. When a particular skill or knowledge is so deep-rooted, it is easy to forget others do not possess the same, right? When our approach is so instinctive, it is easy to forget others are not afforded the same thinking, right? I have spoken about being transparent with what you do, how you can help and what you bring. I have stressed the importance of walking your client and potential clients through your offering. *We have confidence in those who have confidence in themselves.* Have confidence in yourself and have confidence in what you bring.

Remember you have a skill they don't. Do not overlook anything, even the smallest aspect, which you may deem insignificant. If it's part of the offering, then explain it. I see this time and time again. A client will come up with a figure and wince – they feel it is too expensive and are not comfortable aligning it with their offering. Can you relate to this? A sticking-point for many business owners is when they themselves could not afford this figure and so they question if it is the right price-tag. Remember you may not be your ideal client and so it is OK if you cannot afford you.

Over to you: Take one of your products or services. Now pull it apart – work out the time it physically takes to complete the job – including time spent with the customer and the behind-the-scenes toil back at the ranch. Cost up your overheads, what you need to purchase to get the job done. Think about the process involved, the time it has taken to learn the skills that enable you deliver the job. It could have taken thirty years to learn something you can now do in thirty minutes. Now think about the value it will bring to the customer, today and in the future. Look back over feedback and testimonials you've received. What difference have past and current customers said your help has made? Write it down. Use this the next time you have an opportunity to bid for a new piece of work. The confident, well-informed presentation will mean your value is not only understood but bought in to by the client.

A real-life example: A client offered a bespoke cookbook service – aimed at helping those with allergies, health issues, no time or just lack of inspiration in the kitchen. The love of cooking and ability to rustle something up from even the bleakest of cupboards had made them forget others simply could not do this. They had walked away from a very successful career in the city and they now needed to make the money work in their business. The years of training and qualifications they had painstakingly achieved were testament to the investment and belief in their offering. BUT when it came to pricing, they really struggled. Their passion meant they went above and beyond, all the extra bits that no one saw, let alone acknowledged. It was time to put a stop to this.

By pulling apart their offering, they actually began to see more value in what they did than ever before. Uncovering and recognising the small things they had overlooked that were time-consuming, but which really made a difference to their clients. They harnessed this new-found approach, crafted a factual account of what they did and re-established how they could help. Their confidence boosted, they now had a script from which to reference when talking potential clients through the offering. They had a real handle on what they did, how they did it and how it could help. And not only that, seeing their value through new glasses, they *quadrupled* their price! They secured a new client, at the new price after their first call. It works. Try it.

What does price really say?

When something is cheap, we question the quality. It is a basic human reaction, instinct if you like. When we need something quick and dirty, like fried chicken and chips after a boozy night out, the cheaper the better. There is no question then on the quality of what we are buying, which probably has more to do with our inebriated state. But the next day, for lunch, would we grab the same meal? I very much doubt it! Our first thought would be 'but what am I really eating for that price'?

Pricing correctly is settling on a figure that is respectful of the product or service being bought whilst still being attractive to potential customers. A key element here is really knowing who your customer is. There may be many interested parties but not all will make a purchase. And you have to be comfortable with this fact. Knowing this will also enlighten you as to who your competitors are. If you are offering a premium service, it would be plain ridiculous for you to be comparing and matching your price to a budget-priced offering for a similar service. How are you signposting your offering through the price tag to indicate the key differences? If your price matches the budget price, potential customers will assume the same low quality as the budget option. Who is the loser here? YOU!

A real-life example: I was having a conversation with a business development manager at a law firm, they expressed how the changes in the market and the nature of how clients bought their services had driven down the price. We discussed how this was a huge challenge. They continued to say how it was a case of 'if you can't beat them, join them' and the firm where they worked too began matching the prices of the budget online competitors. What effect did this have on the business? Profits fell away, staff felt undervalued and the firm faced an uncertain future.

My response? Ultimately, those customers who are price-driven are going to always seek out the cheapest offer – if this is their key deciding factor, we must accept it. We will not change it. Have you heard of the saying 'You get what you pay for'? Well, it is true. Buy cheap, get cheap. And don't get me wrong, I love a bargain – us cockneys always sniff out a good deal. BUT when it comes to some things, you have to stump up the cash.

You've read (and hopefully remembered!) my message from chapter 1: Accept you aren't going to be everyone's cup of tea. I then pointed out it is about having the courage to stand by what you offer as a business AND to communicate what this offer is. If you don't point out the differences, they won't know the difference. You pay more because you get more. Simple.

Lesson: Do not stop acknowledging the value you bring. Be confident and relaxed when informing others. Remember to remind yourself of all the love you pour into your work, the love that makes the end result far superior. Put the right price tag on the right offering. If you do not own your value, it will be stolen from you. Know it. Own it. Communicate it.

Food for thought

Get paid for your value, not just your time.

Increasing your price is not about adding value where there is none. It is about accounting for what you bring to the table. It is confidently and comfortably explaining what you do. No money-mindset bullshit here – it is strategic, honest, value-based pricing. If you do not know your value, no one else will.

10

YOUR BUSINESS IS NOT A CHARITY AND YOU ARE NOT A VOLUNTEER

MAKING SENSE OF IT ALL

So, you've worked out your value, your clients and how you package your offering, now you must ensure that how you price this makes sense – to your clients and your accountant! Jo Davidson, a fellow businesswoman, quoted the name of this chapter and I couldn't have put it more powerfully if I tried. Keep this at the forefront of your mind, always.

Do you know what you earn? When was the last time you did the figures bit? How often do you check your bank balance? Do you feel safe in the knowledge that there is money in your account so you don't delve any deeper? Or are you worried about the amount of money in your account? When you think about how you price, how does it make you feel? When you think about what you earn, how does it make you feel?

Don't risk losing the love

We go into business because we are stupidly passionate about how we can help or are technically great at something. We believe we can do it better than anyone else. No matter how much love we have, the joy it brings us or the drive we have, the money we earn is paramount. If we can't afford to live, to pay our mortgage, our food bill, worrying about where the next pound is coming from, all of that love will begin to dwindle. This makes me immensely sad as I believe there is always a way of earning and earning well. Immensely sad because to see business owners hustle so hard and to genuinely have something very special to offer but then fall out of love with it because they've stuck their head in the sand when it comes to the pricing. No one can continue if they are consistently in the red. This is so stressful and this doesn't have to be you.

Get that commercial cap on

Do not get confused, not all ideas will fly. No matter how passionate you are. I've had bloody loads. And that is why you have to spend time looking at the financial viability of your business. However painful the realisation might be that the figures simply don't add up. To say it petrifies me that business owners don't do this is not an understatement. Like a bull in a china shop they plough forth, without stopping, listening to advice or being practical. I didn't give up and nor should you. Speak to those most financially successful in business: you may not get it right first, second or even third time round. But you will get there. By being objective, commercial and realistic. Sometimes a nip and tuck make it work, other times a full-on face-lift is necessary. And then sometimes you have to admit that no matter how much you polish it, a turd is still a turd!

Don't stumble when you can fly

I hope I haven't lost you and you've been not only reading the chapters before this but actually listening, taking them on board and practically applying them to your business. If so, there should be no risk that you've got this far and are still unsure if your business has legs. Taking a far enough step back from our business often needs the help of an objective opinion. Whether bouncing ideas around over a beer with a fellow business buddy or investing in a mentor, do it! So back to the passion and making sure we're funnelling this down the right path. If you do this right, you really will have every opportunity to fly. Give yourself and your business that chance. Don't cut corners.

A real-life example: A beautiful holistic beauty salon I worked with very early on is a good example of how and why this process is so important. They had opened a year previously and invested a huge amount in their shop, the products they used and the training they undertook to be at the forefront of their industry. Money was tight and they were losing faith. The looks on the business partners' faces when I suggested breaking down each service they provided, all the products they used and how long each service took them. Classic. There were quite a few. The true income generation for each service was not known and this process was going to make this crystal clear. Drawing up a comprehensive list of every service and for each considering:

- **How long does each service take?** This allows you to refine price: service charge – time + product costs = profit. For example: they paid their hairdresser £10 per hour and a cut and colour took three hours PLUS the products used (which totalled £10) but the client only paid £30. Is this cost-effective? No, is the short answer. Two options: get a more efficient hairdresser and/or increase your prices.

- **How many of any one service can you fit in a day?** What are the most profitable services – the ones that take the least time and have fewer overheads (in this case it was products that were used). They were side-tracked with trying to sell higher-priced treatments like luxury facials, but these took far longer (around sixty minutes) and used more higher-priced products. Whereas, a manicure took twenty minutes, and if a bottle of varnish cost £20 to buy and you can do twenty manicures from each bottle, products used totalled £1 in varnish per client. Quicker and cheaper to do. Yes, these figures have been simplified for this example, but you can hopefully see what I mean.

It allowed the owners to understand where they earned their money, what was the most effective way to use their time, how to maximise input from employees, if they needed to seek out cheaper suppliers and where they could earn more. When we knew their profit margins, we were better equipped to package offers that were not only well received by the client but by their bank balance too. Yes, this exercise did take time and effort but four years in they are reaping the rewards of being more informed and more in control.

> **Lesson:** Knowing your figures allows you to maximise your potential earnings. Time is not limitless so always know how to get the best out of every minute. Whatever you do.

Over to you: To the nuts and bolts. Some thoughts on how you worked out your pricing. Three things:

1. How did you work out your pricing? Was it a finger in the air jobby, a price match of a competitor or a considered calculation?
2. Did you take into account all of the overheads that enable you to offer that service? And yes, that does include your time! Whatever you offer, we all have overheads. Yes, sometimes we can be exact, and sometimes it has to be a 'guesstimation'. Anything is better than not knowing at all.
3. Are you making a profit? It can be a brutal process but sticking your head in the sand, thinking the price sounds good without working out what you are actually taking home, will bite you in the arse at some point. Take control and inform yourself.

Food for thought

Don't let others validating their own financial woes let you think that's just the way it is. Get in to good habits early. Never settle in business. I get so fucking frustrated when I hear 'oh well, my type of business just isn't easy to make a profit in' that 'it's just the way it is'. Bullshit. Make it work and make it work well! It is a choice. Because I wholeheartedly guarantee someone else is making a damn fine profit from the very same thing.

I'm not naive enough to think that if you are opening a business with a commercial unit, the first few months won't be a bit hairy. The money you've thrown at it might outweigh the profits initially. Spend some quality time with your accountant. Know that any investment you make in your business all add up – whether you've got a shiny new office, a delivery van or are working from home. Be realistic (accountants are innate realists) but aim high. If you don't, someone else will.

You deserve to earn and earn well for your graft. Don't deny yourself. And when a client loses sight that we all need to earn money for what we do, ask them if they'd work for free. I find it is a quick way of injecting some perspective for them. My last point, it is OK if money isn't your sole driver, that it is not the reason you get out of bed in the morning. But it does need to be factored in. Always.

Know your financials. Understand what and where you are earning your money. Don't stick your head in the sand. Be brave.

11

BELIEVE AND YOU WILL ACHIEVE

GIVE YOURSELF PERMISSION TO BELIEVE IN YOUR BUSINESS

Sometimes belief is all we have. Sometimes, no-one else around us shares in our belief. It was this belief that instilled the confidence and will to get you to this point in the first place: to become a business owner. Hold on to this belief. Don't let it go, be taken from you, or be lost. It will be this belief that sees you through the darkest, the toughest and the most challenging of times.

Imposter syndrome

I remember feeling like such a fraud when asked what I did for work not long after starting my business. Responding 'I have my own business' felt so grand with immediate perceptions of who I should be, what I should be doing or what I should be like and it felt totally out of reach. I think we all feel like that initially and continue to periodically. We look at those we admire, they really have their shit together, they don't have any bad days where the struggle is real and their belief packs its bags and fucks off. We are wrong, so wrong. This book all along has been about embracing the human side to business. The side where the highs are followed by the lows and the desire to run and hide is strong. But also, the side that makes business fizzle with potential, effervesce with opportunity and sing with success. When we accept it, warts and all, we can make a choice. A choice I talked about at the outset. A choice to let the trying times fuel the good. To learn from the struggles and step forward with that extra knowledge. We are all human, just giving it a go. If you don't give yourself permission to believe, no one else is going to deliver it on a silver platter. Afford yourself that permission. After all, you have to believe in something for it to become something.

Laugh at the doubters

There are two certainties. First, there will be flocks of those who tell you why it won't work, why you are crazy and why you need to find a stable job with a reliable income. With their forehead furrowed and their hands resembling claws, they will say, over and over again, 'Do you not realise how fragile the economy is at the moment and how hard times are just around the corner?' Second, those same individuals will be the ones who moan most about the drudgery of life, how they detest their job, the ones too scared to do something about it. The ones who will use excuses as to why they are unable to muster the courage to do what you have done. I've heard my friend Cassandra Farren say, "You find a way, or you find an excuse." Bloody bang on, Cassie, bang on. Either way, their opinion is null and void. Don't give it any precious time and definitely don't let it cast a shadow on your belief. You have nothing to prove to them. Not now, not ever.

Serious hobbies

I have worked with many business owners who have started a business from a skill that was initially a hobby. This shift in perception, in their own minds, from a bit of fun on the side to a serious money-making business can be difficult. The belief that this could be something they earn a living from and actually enjoy is incomprehensible. If this is you, relish this opportunity, exploit your skillset and remember you will always be one step ahead of your competition. When you love what you do, it shows.

Over to you: Speak to the top athletes about the secret to their successes. They will, of course, acknowledge the graft in training, but what they will always say is that what really gets them through their next race, performance, competition is their own self-belief. That their success largely comes from the mental not the physical strength. I'll leave you with that thought and a quote, one that has genuinely resonated and allowed me to look at my business from a different perspective. As, let's face it, this is a difficult mindset to master for the majority of us. The cartoons really do have some absolute diamonds. Mr Ping from *Kung Fu Panda* said: "To make something special, you have to believe that it is special."

A real-life example: A client who I had been working with for well over a year, was busy launching a sexy new business whilst still pushing the bar in their other well-established, successful business. Their belief in what they do, how they do it and why has recently (and very much deservedly) been acknowledged. At a time when the start-up launch hit squeaky bum territory, they still made the decision to undertake a huge refurbishment in their current business, which saw a total shift in how they worked and what they offered. Most would question the timing, didn't they have enough on? But no, it was this strong belief that drove them forward and a belief that now, not only sets them apart from their competitors, having converted all existing customers to a new service. But ultimately a belief which resulted in their winning 'Business of the Year' award for one of the largest counties in the UK. An accolade that recognised the risk and the beauty of where sheer determination and belief can take you.

> **Lesson:** Yes, another quote! I want you to stop and think on this one, this lesson is short. I love this quote by Ayn Rand: "The question isn't who is going to let me, it's who is going to stop me."

Food for thought

I was recently honoured to be asked to judge at a Sir Jack Petchey Foundation event.It kicked off with some history of the man himself and it was quite moving.

Jack Petchey was born into a working class family in the East End. From a humble background, he grew a business valued at over half a billion pounds. One thing that has stuck with me was his following advice. "To every morning get yourself in front of that mirror —however you may be feeling, whatever the day may have in store — to look yourself in the eye and repeat 'I am an achiever'." The way we perceive ourselves is not only intrinsically linked with the way others perceive us but also stops us limiting our own future accomplishments.

Start as you mean to go on. Believe in yourself, your potential and believe in your business. Try it. Tomorrow. And the next day. And the day after that.

12

THE STRUGGLE IS HARD, KEEP ON HUSTLING

"EVERYTHING WILL BE OK IN THE END. IF IT'S NOT OK IT'S NOT THE END." J. LENNON

No matter how successful you are, what you have achieved or are set to achieve, how well-respected you are or how much money you have – you will have testing times. These times are not talked about enough, they need to be talked about more and you need to know that it is OK for you to feel defeated. You will get through it and there are things you can do to help. Getting your mindset right, however you do it, is key in the bad times as much as in the good.

Not for the faint-hearted

Running your own show may from the outside look easy but I can assure you it's as far from that as is physically possible. Yes, we get to choose our hours of work, but if we aren't grafting, we ain't earning. Something our employed friends overlook.

Who pushes your buttons?

If motivating ourselves every day to keep on keeping on wasn't hard enough, you have to fight off those button-pushers. You know the ones who make you totally lose your shit. The ones that let you down in ways you could never have expected. The ones that knife you in the back as soon as it is turned. The ones you invest in heavily for them to merrily piss it back in your face. I've had it all. Dealing with them in a way that limits the impact on not only you as an individual, but on your business, can be trying.

I have lost count of the times a fellow business owner has said, 'Shit, I had no idea it'd be this hard. I mean I knew it would be tough, but this tough?' Everyone has different ways of getting through those weeks that require copious amounts of wine and/or lots of long walks. Instead of isolating yourself, reach out to someone who understands, another business owner. I will 100% guarantee they have some nuggets of wisdom to share that will help or, at the very least, just getting it off your chest will allow you to stop festering. One thing I know is that however awful it may seem, sleeping on it will bring renewed vigour and an alternative perspective. We need to smile; decide the only control those button-pushers have over you is how you react. Choose to learn and walk. Humans can often do things we least expect, however hard that can be to swallow at the time. Take a deep breath. You will then be better placed to move forward.

A **real-life example:** I remember in the very early days I invested heavily in a contact I respected, trusted and saw the possibility of developing a collaborative relationship with. I'd shared everything from the way I worked to information about my personal life. To say I was devastated when they decided to totally change their service and begin offering what I did was an understatement. To find out they had let me warm up potential clients and then sweep in and offer what I had, and for FREE, was a solid uppercut to the ribs. I cried. I shouted. But mostly I was disappointed. I realised that as cruel as it was experiencing this so early on, it taught me so much. It taught me how to deal with it for when it happens again. What really helped me? I called a fellow business friend and they asked me how I would advise a friend to deal with the situation. This enabled me to step back, lose the emotion and get my business brain back in gear. I knew what I had to do. I called the button-pusher and put them back in their fucking box but in a very professional and succinct way of course! I was not going to sit quietly and smile sweetly. It's not my style anyway. For that individual, their actions backfired and in time I saw their business struggle. Their clients deserted them as they could not provide the service they had promised. I do not like to see others struggle but sometimes we all have to learn the hard way. My lesson here was that people can try to copy you, emulate your offering but they'll never be you. And they will always get found out. Eventually.

Over to you: Have you identified your go-to people for times like this? The ones who you may not necessarily class as friends, but you know who 'get it', when friends and family just don't – they may not have ever dreamed let alone dared to start their own business. Don't make the mistake of isolating yourself. Do you network? Get out regularly and mix with like-minded individuals? A major benefit of networking means you build a team of supporters, supporters who have walked in your shoes and trodden your path. These fellow business buddies are priceless in times of crisis. Don't overlook them and deny yourself this lifeline.

Lesson: Sometimes all you can do is laugh at the struggle. Know it will get better and, as long as you learn from it, it will only benefit you in the future. This quote raises a smile on my face on even the toughest of days: "When you thought it would be easy peasy lemon squeezy but it's actually difficult difficult, lemon difficult".

Food for thought

It's true when they say no one sees the struggle they just see the success. The years of graft, blood, sweat and tears. The nearly giving up. The being put through the ringer time and again. Getting knocked down and having to find the strength from somewhere to get back on your feet. The struggle is real. I want to end on this quote as a shout out to all of you. A shout out for now and in the future. Don't give up.

"Shout out to everyone making progress that no one recognises because you never let anyone see the dark moments. You've been silently winning battles and transforming yourself, be proud of every step you're making in the right direction. Keep going because you've got this". – Unknown.

13

BE KIND TO YOURSELF AND THOSE AROUND YOU

"EVERY DAY MAY NOT BE GOOD BUT THERE IS GOOD IN EVERYDAY" – UNKNOWN

Dispelling a myth

Kindness in business, does it even exist? ABSO-FUCKING-LUTELY! Being aware of your own and others needs in business will make you a force to be reckoned with. Why? Because being compassionate is too often overlooked but never forgotten. No, my business-brain and commercial-mindedness has not disappeared. But I do think for all of us in business, kindness is king.

Humanity starts at home

If as business owners we don't look after ourselves, we cannot possibly do our best by our business or our clients. Cutting ourselves some slack every now and again should not be an inconvenience but a necessity. If we do not show ourselves the same respect as we show others how can we expect to get the best out of ourselves?

A real-life example: It's no coincidence that I'm writing this chapter on World Kindness Day. Nor that I've had multiple reminders this week to be kinder to myself. I am not going to lie, this week has been bloody tough, in lots of different ways.

As I sit here writing, I have a full bag of beauties to tackle. I'm six months pregnant and I feel like the countdown has begun, not only to meeting bubba but to me getting my business and myself in the best possible place before this little person joins the family. To maintain momentum, keep relationships strong, clients happy and forge new exciting collaborations. To make damn sure the business I have been nurturing and building for three years is waiting when I return. To pursue passion projects that I care about deeply, to finish writing this book (I hope it's obvious just how much I've loved writing every word), to mentoring young people at risk of homelessness and to delivering a project that will support and give a voice to pregnant women.

Personally, the fact Christmas is only six weeks away makes things slightly more tense. That I'm trying to get my five gym training sessions in a week (I'm a massive advocate of the positive effects exercise brings to all aspects of our lives) despite being ill for the last month. To make sure my house is ticking along, and I don't lose my head trying to make it perfect for bubba. To be a good wife. A supportive daughter. A fun friend. To be happy.

This is just a snapshot of what's currently on my plate. We all have overcrowded plates and not the good type of overcrowded like one of my nan's classic roasts (come on, you must have been expecting a food mention somewhere in this chapter!). Sometimes it's time to offload. And to know it's OK if you can't juggle everything. I know if I haven't got the headspace, I won't be happy with the end-result. So, popping things on pause is the best solution. I'm trying to be kinder to myself. Be kinder to yourself too.

The guilt-trip

Over to you: Self-compassion, is this something you are familiar with? When you have accepted that you are not godlike and that in fact you do need a break, that you do need to rest. The guilt around stepping away from your business and your clients, for whatever reason, can be overwhelming. Just a few little reminders for you, just in case you need them:

It is OK *if your head just isn't in the game and you are currently unable to be your usual sparkly self. When we are employed, we accept that there will be times that our energy is depleted and we slow down for a while – why should it be any different now?*

It is OK *if you are having doubts about the direction of your business- given some time away all will become clear.*

It is **OK** *if you are unwell and need to cancel an engagement or client – be honest and give them as much notice as possible.*

It is **OK** *if all of your confidence has deserted you and you want to hide under a large duvet. It happens to the best of us. It will pass.*

It is **OK** *if you are going on holiday and won't be contactable – recharging those batteries properly requires complete shutdown. Think how much quicker our phone recharges if it is switched off. Just give everyone advance warning and put that bleeping bugger in a drawer.*

It is **OK** *if life is throwing you shit-covered balls and you simply haven't got the emotional or physical strength to get your usual jazz hands out. Be truthful with those you may have pre-made plans; their sympathy may surprise you. If they aren't understanding, I would question if you even wanted to work with them anyway.*

Dealing with the life that happens around your business *can be a real challenge. It is OK to be affected by it.*

Lesson: How we talk to ourselves and how we talk to others we care about, in a business or personal setting, goes a long way. Can you remember when someone last showed you kindness, not because they had to but because they chose to? How did it make you feel? When was the last time you were kind to yourself? Allowed yourself that time out. Gave yourself permission to acknowledge that it was OK if the life happening around you disrupted your business. Accepted that you couldn't possibly always be firing on all cylinders. Dared to show your vulnerabilities. Recognised that you weren't superhuman.

Food for thought

When we are kinder to ourselves it allows us to be kinder to those around us.

In business, applying some extra thought to how you work, how you speak and how you support others makes you unforgettable. It makes you irreplaceable. Be irreplaceable.

A friend, Heather Prince, put it perfectly: *"Being kind hardly costs a thing. You'll hardly remember you did it. But the other person will never forget that you did."*

14

THE SMALLEST STEPS
MAKE THE
BIGGEST DIFFERENCE

NEVER FORGET HOW FAR YOU HAVE COME

Do you feel stuck to the spot? Are you moving, but not in the direction you wanted? Do you feel like you are moving backwards? Are your sideway steps frustrating your progress?

A step is still a step

Whatever direction you are moving, and yes sometimes we do have to step back to move forward – as long as you're moving, it is positive – the smallest of steps can make the hugest of strides. Strides which may not necessarily be fruitful immediately but give them time. An apple tree may only bear fruit every two years but when they do, it will be a better-quality harvest. Be patient. We can underestimate how long things take to happen and our path to achieving them. As long as you don't stay still, apart from when you are taking a moment to pause to reflect, and assess the best way forth. When we stagnate, we lose our focus, our momentum and our purpose. Do not panic if you can feel yourself slipping in to state-stagnate – call on someone your trust to help you shake it off and regain state-action.

Making each step count

When we are faced with a task that stops us in our tracks what should we do? We need to reinstate some control and feel confident about our next step. With so much happening at any one time, our brains are pulled in a million different directions. It is about finding a way to pull it all back to the nuts and bolts – the sounding board we all need to bounce off every so often.

This is where I remind you of what I shared in the very first chapter. The bit about the business values – the pegs that keep your business where it should be. If you haven't done it, do it now. If you have done it, now is the time to revisit them. These values pull us back in line – when needed – and it is these values that also reaffirm our decisions. They are the best, most useful tool we have to keep us, not only on track, but to give us clarity in what is the best next move.

When a client comes to me because they feel lost in a directionless fog, I can be met by a puzzled face when I ask them about their values. Whatever the situation – creating a more rigorous plan for the business, securing a big win, working out how best to market your business – revisit those values. Without clarity we cannot possibly feel in control and without being in control how on earth can we hope to be making the right decisions to enable our business to thrive? I hope all the different sections are neatly slotting in to place and you can see how they are all linked and how they all have a huge impact on how you run your business.

Honesty it always the best policy

A real-life example: A conversation I had with a new client and the best way forward to help them with pricing. They were honest about not knowing where to begin and admitted they were just avoiding it. I didn't judge them; I respected their honesty and because of this we were able to get to work creating a positive solution in a much shorter time-frame. I love it when I work with people that are assured enough to put their hand up and say, 'That area just isn't my strength.' In business, it is just as important to be as assertive in what we can't do, as what we can. It saves time and money. My first thoughts were about the values of their business and how they are intrinsically linked with how we value ourselves and how we price our offering. It is these values that we need to revisit to get a proper grip on how we breakdown the blocks stopping this business owner moving forward. Reminding themselves allows the client to immediately feel back in the driving seat and a path forward begins to emerge from the fog. It is then about setting realistic and practical steps to get us to our destination. Et voila.

Top Tip: When we are honest, with ourselves and those whose help we need, we get to where we need to be far quicker.

Knowing it is the right step

Our paths can be ever-changing and there can be many we have to tread at the same time. So how do we know where our next step should be, what direction it should be in and if it is the right step at all? When we are focused on just getting to a particular place, smashing a goal, launching a new product, how we actually get there can be daunting – a feel-our-way-as-we-go approach or a stagnate-inducing deer in headlights moment. How can we make this not only easier but more efficient? By sitting down and giving it some practical thought.

When I write business plans, I describe them as to-do lists. They aren't pages long but instead allow the reader, the business owner, to quickly get up to speed and work out what they need to do next. They feature plenty of small tasks and it is these small steps that amount to that one unreachable objective. It always amazes me that when I am feeling like I'm standing at the bottom of a very tall wall, if I stop trying to scramble up it aimlessly and break it down how a workable route appears. Like the ski instructors say, 'wind down the hill: it puts you in control of the slope instead of heading straight down at breakneck speed and it controlling you'. Did you hear that word control again?

Over to you: Put yourself in control. Take the time to stop and work it out. What is your next goal, how can you break it down to create achievable steps that are realistic within your day-to-day schedule? Add a timeframe to them, to give you some accountability. What do you want to achieve in the next month, the next quarter, the next year? Give yourself a to do list, work out a plan and yes these will include delegating to others better placed with the task in hand!

Lesson: We all have lofty ambitions, and so we should, but we do not reach them without taking the right steps. Think about when you are cooking something for the first time. You could compare the ingredients to who needs to support you to reach your end goal, and the method as a business plan. Without either we would have nothing to show at the end of our toil. But it is also the small steps, the when to pop in that teaspoon of water, that creates something really special at the end.

Food for thought

Thinking of that teaspoon of water: the smallest and often the simplest of steps can be the ones that are fundamental in reaching the end purpose. Do not overlook these steps, even half-steps. They all add up and when you look back and see how far you have come you will be amazed. A bit like when you open the oven and see that your cake has risen (mmmmm, cake!). Do not wait to get to that end goal to pat yourself on the back, you will have something else to focus on then and what happens is we never end up celebrating anything.

We are so ardently looking ahead, for the next big thing, we never look back. Looking back reminds us of all we have achieved that we never thought possible. Looking back reminds us we can do this. Looking back reminds us we are doing this. Looking back gives us the belief and fortitude to look to the future. Celebrate as many steps and milestones along the way as you can. Take some time out and raise a glass to you. You deserve it, you've worked so hard.

15

YOU ARE THE DIFFERENCE

YOUR BUSINESS ON YOUR TERMS

Do you feel conflicted about what you currently offer versus what you would like to offer? Do you feel that the joy you envisaged when you did you own thing is lacking? Do you feel unsure of your product or service? Are you not particularly fond of some of your clients?

Let's get one thing straight

Enjoying what you do and who you do it with does NOT mean you are work shy. You are allowed to enjoy your work, otherwise I would be questioning what it was all for? Every time I speak to a client or a fellow business owner and they say they want to enjoy what they do, they immediately feel as though they have to qualify this statement. Qualify it by saying, 'I am not saying I'm not willing to work hard.' Why is it that we all immediately think that if we enjoy something it isn't hard work? I will tell you why, because when we enjoy what we do, it doesn't feel like hard work, well not in the same way anyway. Let me distinguish this more in your mind with a quote. A quote from my calisthenic coach: "*Working hard for something we don't care about is called stress. Working hard for something we love is called passion."* I implore you, please, if you don't enjoy what you are doing – after all the strength you have mustered to go at it alone – make a change.

Sustained success

How do you make sure you are jumping out of bed each day? Okay, so there may be some days where you hit the snooze button, but how will you keep these to a minimum? Putting yourself first in your business can feel self-indulgent. We've already talked about this, but it is vital to give your business the oxygen it needs to keep on breathing. Reflect on what you have achieved, and what you have learned. Make a commitment to yourself to keep on doing some things. Make a commitment to yourself to scrap others who may not be serving you financially or mentally. Make a commitment to begin doing things that you have kept on the back burner, recognising that it is now time to action and that this will have potential to both reinvigorate you and your business. Bring the business back to you, the individual behind it all. Don't run yourself into the ground working with clients that make you miserable. Create a business on your terms. Create a business that makes you happy. Create a business that doesn't leave you broken. Because, after all, without you, there is no business.

Going-it alone

It is important to address the fears, the insecurities and the perceived shortcomings we may have when we set up our own business. If we have always been part of a big business, with a global reputation, we can believe that these factors are the defining reason why we are chosen over a competitor. That it is *not* the individual that is sent from the big business that seals the deal, but the brand they work for instead. I have mentioned how we can never dictate who buys us and why and yes, sometimes work is won simply down to reputation. However, we are seeing a huge shift in this – much like online purchasing. Consumers want a personal, bespoke service – they want to feel valued. A type of service the big boys just can't provide in all cases. Do not think that as a solopreneur you can't get these mammoth corporates shaking in their boots because you very much can! You have something they simply do not – you are nimble, flexible, not stymied by red tape and ready to build a lasting relationship with your client. You are in control of how you help them and in what way, and that, my friend, makes you a serious threat.

A real-life example: *A client, for their whole career, had worked for large internationally-renowned consultancy firms. Although they knew they were good, very good, at what they did, and it was this skill that had brought huge accreditation to the firms where they worked, they worried about how they would win work on setting* *up their own business. At the very beginning of our working together, exploring particular areas of focus for their business, they shared with me a 'win story'. It had been for a huge governmental project that everyone wanted to win. They had turned up to pitch for the work, on their own, no flashy marketing presentation (apologies to all my fellow marketing professionals) but just as themselves. Indeed, whilst waiting to be called in they did notice the teams sent by competing firms running through their perfectly curated presentations. There was no turning back. Long story short: they won the work. Why? Because their personal, non-fussy approach was refreshing. They were chosen because they had turned up as themselves and the client was able to actually talk to the person who would be doing the job – not someone merely representing the do-er. The client immediately felt comforted, with a sense of trust, and this kicked the relationship off to a great start. Yes, whilst my client won this work they were still part of an international consultancy, but it was quite clear that this was not the reason they were chosen. It was also no surprise the client followed them when they went out alone. A pertinent message there, do you not agree?*

Over to you: This is an opportunity to look or ask for feedback as to why a client chooses to work with you. These reasons will be far-reaching, and they will surprise you. You are the difference. In terms of how you work, you set the rules, nobody else. Whilst being the captain of our ships can at times be a bit hairy, particularly when you feel engulfed by the mammoth waves, it can also be exhilarating, having the freedom to follow the wind into uncharted, opportunistic territories. No one to stop you or hold you back. Make sure you are making the most of this freedom: when you feel you are being buffeted in the wrong direction, switch that sail and change course.

Lesson: A reminder for you all. Your reputation is yours and yours alone. Your expertise and credibility are yours and yours alone. Your past, current and future successes are yours and yours alone. No matter where you have worked before, or are currently working, there will not be a bloody huge rubber that comes and erases all of your professional history. You own that shit. It is nobody else's, just yours.

Food for thought

A fellow business mentor, Leigh Howes, put it simply, *"It is not just about building a business. It is about building a business that you want to be a part of."*

So, if you are feeling conflicted about what you offer, address it. Offer what you want to offer, not what you think you should or what your competitors are offering. Regain that joy, remember your 'why'. Have a watertight assurance in your offering. It is only you that can say how much grief you are willing to take from your clients – but set a limit and stick to it.

When you love what you do, it shows. People will want to work with you. When it works for you it will work for others also.

16

WHAT DOES SUCCESS
LOOK LIKE TO YOU?

KNOW IT AND BE TRUE TO IT

You see I feel there is an inherent issue with chasing success and this is largely because most of us can fall into the trap of chasing somebody else's idea of it. What it is, what it feels like and what you will feel like when you reach it. Like the perfect meal, we wouldn't expect ours to be the same as somebody else's – but why do we do the same with success? So, what happens? Well, we chase a concept of success, a concept that we haven't really explored, questioned or understood. We feel like we are chasing something and never quite reaching it.

What guise does it take for you?

Endless money or just enough so there isn't any worry. Being happy or not being totally miserable? Having a 'healthy' (what healthy means to one is something very different to another) balance with work and your private life? Being liked or being respected? Being feared or being approachable? Influencing change or being under the radar? Having good health, good friends and a happy family?

Words cut deep

A real-life example: I remember when my dad turned around to me about five years ago and said, 'You know what, Sarah-Jane, I really thought you were going to be more successful.' Safe to say that fucking stung like a bloody big bee. My first reaction was to inform him on what I actually did for a job, as he had no idea. He had no idea how tough it was working in the corporate world, as he had never worked within it. He had run a a thriving family business for forty-five years. He had no concept of what it felt like to be a woman, holding her own and being respected, in a male-dominated environment. He had not stuck by his guns and fought against the status quo to have a voice, to get back up when he'd been knocked down. He had not lived my life, nor my career and was completely ill-informed.

> **Lesson:** My point here is to not make this a woe is me story but to share a deeply personal disappointment and come out thinking – you have no fucking clue. And to be damn clear on how others' perception of what success looks like should have no bearing on how we perceive it, what we aim for, or how we live. Our success is ours, and ours only. No matter who is commenting, even the closest, they do not have any bearing on what it could or should look like.

Over to you: What does success look like to you, for you? How does it feel? How does it make you feel? You may like to spend some time reflecting on this, however you reflect best. In a world where we are often dictated to what success is, what we must all strive for, it can be really hard to work out what the hell it means to us. And then when we have worked it out, to have the assurance to actually share it. Sadly, I cannot tell you how to work this one out, it's one for you and your intuition I am afraid – being truthful about what feels right.

Money mindset

I mentioned much earlier in the book that my focus on money and what I earned changed dramatically when I stepped away from the City. Thinking specifically of a money mindset workshop I attended (which mirrored many conversations I'd had), the main thrust was to put your energy behind a figure and that would enable you to earn it over the forthcoming month. I sat thoroughly uncomfortable throughout, but not really knowing why I felt so uneasy. What I reflected on and eventually understood was, in fact, pretty obvious. I didn't get out of bed, nor be driven by how much I earned because that was so far from what success looked like to me. Earning and earning well was a fantastic by-product of being good at what I did. And to be good at what I did I had to genuinely care about, not only who I worked with, but the integrity of the business I was building. Success to me was being trusted and respected enough for someone to trust me with advising them about their baby – their business. That meant more than any sum of money. Yes, others disregarded my version of success, even mocked it. I smiled and ignore them. Truth is, whatever it means to you is for no one else to comment on. Which also means it is for no one else to assess your success on their terms. Whoever it is.

Food for thought

Remember, depending on the day, the time in your life or the stage of your business, success can look very different. If I think of what my clients have said, it ranges from being taken seriously as a business owner, being respected as a professional within a given field, being understood by customers and peers, making a positive difference to people and their lives, not having to worry about money anymore, or having to supplement being self-employed with stints in employed positions. I could go on.

It is imperative that in business we celebrate each and every one with a clap on the back, a quiet moment to enjoy it and/or a glass of something nice. One day it can be just getting out of bed. Another could be pushing yourself further out of your comfort zone than you ever thought possible. Alternatively, it could be winning that million-pound contract! It could also be you saying no, when you'd have ordinarily said yes. It could be finally setting up your blog. It could be getting your online accounts sorted out. I think you get the picture now!

I want to leave you safe in the knowledge that whatever it looks like for you, it is all good. Know it, own it and be true to it. Go forth, Be fearless. Have fun!

Be more successful in business by being you.

Good business comes from the people behind it.

Love

SJ x

"It's always darkest before the dawn."

Proverb

CONTACT ME

I hope you have enjoyed reading this book and found it useful.

Please message me if you have any questions, would like to offer feedback or if you need any help with your business.

WRITE: sj@meowconsulting.co.uk

FOLLOW: @meowconsulting on Instagram

Printed in Great Britain
by Amazon

52437524R00093